# SNOWY OWLS

by Melissa Hill

a Capstone company — publishers for children

Raintree is an imprint of Capstone Global Library Limited, a company incorporated in England
and Wales having its registered office at 7 Pilgrim Street, London, EC4V 6LB – Registered
company number: 6695582

www.raintree.co.uk
myorders@raintree.co.uk

Editorial Credits
Jeni Wittrock, editor; Juliette Peters, designer; Morgan Walters, media researcher;
Katy LaVigne, production specialist

ISBN 978 1 4747 0496 0
20 19 18 17 16
10 9 8 7 6 5 4 3 2 1

British Library Cataloguing in Publication Data
A full catalogue record for this book is available from the British Library.

Photo Credits
Corbis: Kennan Ward, 17; Dreamstime: Brian Kushner, 9; Getty Images: mlorenzphotography, 22, Thomas Kokta,
15; Glow Images: ARCO/Wiede/U. & M., 19, Glenn Bartley, 5; iStockphoto: bikec, (inset) 1; Science Source: Annie
Haycock, 21; Shutterstock: Artography, (mossy bark texture) cover and throughout, (red bark texture) 3, 7, Dmitri
Gomon, (snowy owl) bottom left 3, Eric Isselee, (parakeet) bottom right 6, Iakov Filimonov, (owl) bottom left 6, J.
Helgason, (tree stump) back cover, 2, 24, LesPalenik, cover, Maxim Petrichuk, (mountain landscape) 1, 2, 23, 24,
MyImages-Micha, 7, Paul Tessier, 11, Stawek, (map) 8; SuperStock: Bruce J Lichtenberge/Alaska Stock-Design Pics, 13

Printed in China

# Contents

# Great white owls

A white owl with big, yellow eyes lands in the snow. Thick feathers keep its feet and body warm. It's a snowy owl.

Snowy owls are large.

Females can weigh more than

2.7 kilograms (6 pounds).

Males are smaller.

**Size comparison**

snowy owl
length:
51–71 centimetres
(20–28 inches)

budgie
length:
15–20 centimetres
(6–8 inches)

# Snowy homes

Snowy owls begin their lives in the Arctic Circle. They are also found in Europe, North America and Asia.

North America

Europe

Asia

Africa

South America

Australia

where snowy owls live

# Hidden hunters

In snowy places, white feathers help snowy owls to hide. They do not want their prey to see them. The owls' camouflage works well.

A hungry snowy owl listens for prey. Swoop! The owl's strong feet and sharp talons grab its prey. Snowy owls eat lemmings, voles and other rodents.

If food is hard to find, snowy owls fly south. They may fly 3,219 kilometres (2000 miles) or more. In spring they return to the Arctic Circle.

# Arctic families

In the Arctic, females scratch a nest into the land. They lay up to nine white eggs. A month later, snowy owl chicks hatch.

Young snowy owls have fluffy

white and grey feathers.

Snowy owls take good care

of their growing chicks.

After four months, the chicks can fly and hunt. As adults they will start families of their own. In the wild, snowy owls live for about 10 years.

# GLOSSARY

**Arctic Circle** area around the North Pole

**camouflage** colouring or pattern that helps an animal to blend in with the things around it

**chick** young owl

**hatch** break out of an egg

**prey** animal that is hunted by other animals

**predator** animal that hunts other animals

**rodent** one of a group of small mammals with large front teeth for chewing

**talon** long, sharp claw

# READ MORE

*Bird Babies* (Animal Babies), Catherine Veitch (Raintree, 2014)

*Birds* (Animal Classification), Angela Royston (Raintree, 2015)

*Owl vs Mouse* (Predator vs Prey), Mary Meinking Chambers (Raintree, 2012)

# WEBSITES

BBC Nature: all about snowy owls

*www.bbc.co.uk/nature/life/Snowy_Owl*

RSPB: bird guide

*www.rspb.org.uk/discoverandenjoynature/discoverandlearn/birdguide/*

# COMPREHENSION QUESTIONS

1. Why are snowy owls' feathers important?

2. Why do you think female snowy owls are larger than males?

# INDEX